Jean Chrétien

The scrapper who climbed his way to the top

Written by Nate Hendley
Illustrated by Gabriel Morrissette

© 2005 JackFruit Press Ltd.
Publisher — Jacqueline Brown
Editor — Annie Jacobsen
Designer and Art Director — Marcel Lafleur
Researcher — Barbara Baillargeon

JackFruit Press Ltd.
Toronto, Canada
www.jackfruitpress.com

Library and Archives Canada Cataloguing in
Publication

Hendley, Nate, 1966–
Jean Chrétien: The scrapper who climbed his
way to the top / written by Nate Hendley;
illustrated by Gabriel Morrissette.

Includes index.
ISBN 0-9736406-6-9

1. Chrétien, Jean, 1934–   . —Juvenile
literature. 2. Canada—Politics and
government—1993–   . —Juvenile literature.
3. Prime ministers–Canada–Biography–
Juvenile literature. I. Morrissette, Gabriel,
1959–   . II. Title.
FC636.C47H45 2005
j971.064'8'092
C2005-905349-6

Printed and bound in Canada

Commerce Press Inc

JackFruit Press gratefully acknowledges the
support of its printer, Commerce Press Inc,
www.cpress.ca.

Contents

Hot topics

Jean Chrétien: Canada's

Jean Chrétien likes to call himself "the little guy," but Canada's 20th prime minister is actually quite tall (188 centimetres, or 6 feet 2). And he's anything but a small fry in Canadian politics. He is Canada's rowdiest PM—tough, aggressive, and happy to use his fists just about any time.

rowdiest prime minister

He called himself *le petit gars de Shawinigan* (the little guy from Shawinigan), but he was anything but a little guy in Canadian politics.

He was Canada's rowdiest prime minister—tough, aggressive, and happy to use his fists. He once grabbed an angry protester around the neck and pushed him to the ground. He also had to defend himself against an armed intruder who broke into his house in the middle of the night. As the 18th of 19 children, he'd learned to defend himself!

An unlikely politician

Jean Chrétien overcame a number of disabilities and disadvantages. He was deaf in one ear. When he was 12 years old, his face became partially paralyzed. He also has a learning disability that affects the way he speaks and causes him to stumble over his words. When he first entered Parliament, he could barely speak

English; French was his first language, but his critics claimed his French was no better than his English. He has the dubious honour of being the only prime minister to be misunderstood in both of Canada's official languages! His family had little money and he was raised in a small town far away from centres of power.

None of this mattered to Jean. He was determined to make his mark. First he became a lawyer, then a **member of Parliament**, then a **cabinet minister**, and, finally, leader of the **Liberal party**. He helped to bring Canada's **constitution** home and he helped to keep Canada together by convincing Quebecers to vote—on two separate occasions—to stay as part of Canada. He refused to bow to political pressures and kept Canadian troops out of the US invasion of Iraq in 2002. As this military intervention spiralled into an endless series of conflicts, many Canadians agreed that Jean's decision not to participate had been wise.

Jean brought order to Canada's finances and strengthened the economy. Critics sometimes accused him of being wishy-washy (indecisive), but voters liked what they saw and gave him the distinction of being the only Canadian prime minister to have three **majority governments** in a row.

Through it all, Jean had his childhood sweetheart, **Aline Chaîné**, by his side. Although she was not often on centre stage, he called her his best adviser.

A game of survival

Ever the scrapper, Jean was always ready to defend himself against anyone who made fun of him or who didn't agree with his ideas. This was true of him both as a child and as an adult. He had little time for people he saw as wimps and whiners.

"The art of politics," he said in his 1985 autobiography, "is learning to walk with your back to the wall, your elbows high, and a smile on your face. It's a survival game played under the glare of lights. If you don't learn that, you're quickly finished. It's damn tough and you can't complain; you just have to take it and give it back.

"The press wants to get you. The Opposition wants to get you. Even some of the bureaucrats want to get you. They may all have an interest in making you look bad and they all have ambitions of their own."

Want to know more? The words in bold are explained in the glossary at the back of the book.

School-age Ti-Jean is hyperactive and talks constantly. He is sensitive about his small size and about being deaf in his right ear. Anyone who makes fun of him gets pushed back.

Just as he has done on so many other occasions, Jean uses his fists to fend off a bully who's been bugging him. Needless to say, the priests who run his school aren't exactly pleased.

The hellraiser from Shawinigan

Joseph Jacques Jean Chrétien was born on January 11, 1934, the 18th of 19 children. His father, Wellie, was a machinist at a paper mill and his mother, Marie Boisvert-Chrétien, was a warm and loving woman who supported Jean through thick and thin. Only nine of Wellie and Marie's children survived childhood, unfortunate but typical for the time. Because the Chrétiens had already had a son named Jean (*Gros Jean*, "Big John") who had died, they called the second Jean, who was tiny, *Ti-Jean* (short for *Petit Jean*).

Rugged beauty spoiled by noise and pollution

La Baie Shawinigan, the village where Ti-Jean grew up, was primarily French Catholic. It was situated beside the larger city of Shawinigan, a thriving metropolis of 25,000 people of both English and French descent.

The rugged beauty of Shawinigan was spoiled by pulp-and-paper mills, factories, and power plants generating non-stop noise and air pollution. Almost all the men in town, including Wellie, worked at either a mill or a plant.

An unpopular position

Ti-Jean was born into a feisty and politically active family. Wellie was a human dynamo. In addition to his machinist position, he also held part-time jobs to support his family. He was a member of the Liberal party when being a Liberal meant that you were opposed to the huge presence of the Catholic Church in education and everyday life. This was not a popular position in Quebec at the time. Jean's grandfather, François Chrétien, was nearly kicked out of the Catholic Church for walking out during a sermon in which the priest attacked Liberal prime minister **Sir Wilfrid Laurier**.

Wellie was a strong supporter of Canada. He'd seen what had happened to French Canadians who'd gone to New England and been absorbed into American society—they'd lost their language, culture, and beliefs.

Wellie and Marie were also big believers in education, which made them stand out in a town where brute strength and hockey were prized above intelligence. When Ti-Jean was five years old, he was shipped off to a boarding school called Jardin de l'Enfance. He hated the strict discipline and badly wanted to go to a regular school and live at home, but Wellie wouldn't bend. He believed that boarding school would be good for his son, who was already gaining a reputation as a pretty wild kid.

Quick to use his fists

Ti-Jean couldn't sit still and talked constantly. He was sensitive about his small size and about being deaf in his right ear. And he was quick to use his fists whenever anyone bugged him. Needless to say, the priests who ran his school weren't exactly pleased.

Jean's mother, Marie, did her best to encourage him and set him on the right path, but his father was a tough, silent figure who rarely complimented his children.

Jean spent six years at Jardin de l'Enfance, fighting, fuming, and occasionally learning something. His family saw him as a troublemaker and wondered how to control the rascally Ti-Jean.

Bell's palsy

On a brutally cold day in February 1946, 12-year-old Jean walked to a church where his sister, Giselle, was getting married. When he got to the church, the left side of his face was frozen. To his mother's horror, his face remained partly paralyzed for weeks. Frostbite may have brought on a condition known as Bell's palsy. The left side of Jean's face remained permanently crooked.

The timing couldn't have been worse. Jean was about to be sent to another boarding school called Joliette. This school had an excellent reputation but was also ultra-strict. Wellie hoped that the excellence would rub off on his son. But Jean had other ideas.

When he was 15, he came up with what he thought was a very cool plan to escape Joliette. Another student had suffered from appendicitis (a painful swelling of the appendix) and Jean knew how to fake all the

J ean became interested in politics when he was 12. He and his siblings helped their dad by passing out Liberal party pamphlets and setting up chairs at political meetings in town.

What is a learning disability?

Disabilities can be hard to talk about, especially for someone who actually has one. But being open about such things is a good idea, because the more you know, the better you can handle any challenges that come from it.

There are many kinds of disabilities, some visible, others invisible. Visible ones include someone missing an arm or using a wheelchair. Invisible disabilities are harder to recognize. Some can be genetic, others the result of an illness or injury that has affected a person's body or mind in a way that changes the way he or she lives, behaves, or thinks. Learning disabilities make it harder for someone to learn things the way the rest of us do.

Attention Deficit Disorder: this is a disability that many people have, but it can be hard to diagnose. Kids affected by it have trouble keeping their attention on a specific task, like reading a book. They can also seem unusually active or impulsive. They often feel the urge to do something different every minute of the day.

Dyslexia: a common learning disability that affects 5–15 per cent of the population. In some cases, dyslexia makes it hard for a person to read black text on white paper. Others have trouble adding or subtracting (though those same people might be able to solve complex mathematical questions). Jean Chrétien has a form of speech dyslexia called "dysphasia" that makes him use the wrong words in a sentence or makes his words come out in the wrong order.

Fetal Alcohol Syndrome: it is suspected that Michel Chrétien, Jean's adopted son, is one of many Canadians who have to cope with this disability. The permanent brain damage happens before a child is born, and is caused by the mother drinking alcohol while she is pregnant. This condition can affect a person in many ways, like making it difficult for them to understand what is right and what is wrong, to tell the difference between reality and fantasy, or to have trouble remembering things.

Having a learning disability can be difficult, especially in school. But with the right help, opportunities, and support, people with learning disabilities can work through the "invisible" barriers and be very successful. And it is always important to focus on the person, not the disability. Famous people like Albert Einstein, Ludwig von Beethoven, Thomas Edison, and Alexander Graham Bell are all thought to have had some type of learning disability, and they're considered to be some of the greatest minds ever born. And Jean's disability certainly did not stop him from becoming prime minister of Canada.

For more information about learning disabilities, visit our website at www.jackfruitpress.com.

What a way to get a day off school! But Jean's plan backfired...

symptoms. He hunched over and shrieked when the doctors poked and prodded his stomach. Even his older brother, Maurice, who was a doctor, was fooled. The doctors decided to operate. Jean was terrified, but was even more afraid of confessing that he was faking. When the doctors opened him up, they saw that his appendix was healthy but removed it anyway. Maurice covered up what had happened so that Wellie wouldn't know.

Falling in love—twice

Around the time he was recovering from his surgery, Jean fell in love. Twice. First, he became powerfully attracted to politics. He handed out pamphlets at Liberal party rallies and even gave speeches of his own. He was becoming more self-confident. Ti-Jean had shot up to become a tall, gangly teenager.

And politics wasn't the only thing exciting him. In the summer of 1952, when he was 18, he fell in love with a pretty, dark-haired girl named Aline Chaîné.

Aline was soft-spoken, dignified, and quiet—the opposite of the fiery Ti-Jean. Under her influence, Jean settled down and got motivated. By this time, he was attending another boarding school, in Trois-Rivières. Because he wanted to be with Aline and to do something with his life, he started working hard. Finally, he was behaving in a way that pleased the priests who taught him. But Jean was still a fast-talking guy with a lot of friends, still a rebel. He often slipped out of the school at night to hang out with his buddies.

When Jean was 20, his mother died of a heart attack. Jean was devastated. Her death reinforced his decision to shape up and work hard to make his family proud.

A hard-working scrapper

By now, Jean had made up his mind to be a lawyer. After graduating from boarding school, Jean entered Laval University's law school in Quebec City. He quickly became class president and an outspoken Liberal.

At Laval there were parties, pubs, and girls. And Jean was finally free, able to do what he wanted. But he never liked drinking and wasn't interested in any girl but Aline. He went to see her every single weekend and she encouraged him to keep up his studies.

Jean and Aline were married on September 10, 1957. Within a year, Aline gave birth to a daughter. A year later, Jean graduated with a law degree from Laval. Jean and Aline moved back to Shawinigan and Jean joined a local law firm.

Jean went to work early and stayed late. But he was still prone to get into fights. Once, at a meeting of the bar association in Trois-Rivières, a fellow lawyer made some nasty remarks and up went Ti-Jean's fists. The lawyer found himself, bloody and dazed, on the floor. What a scrapper, that Jean!

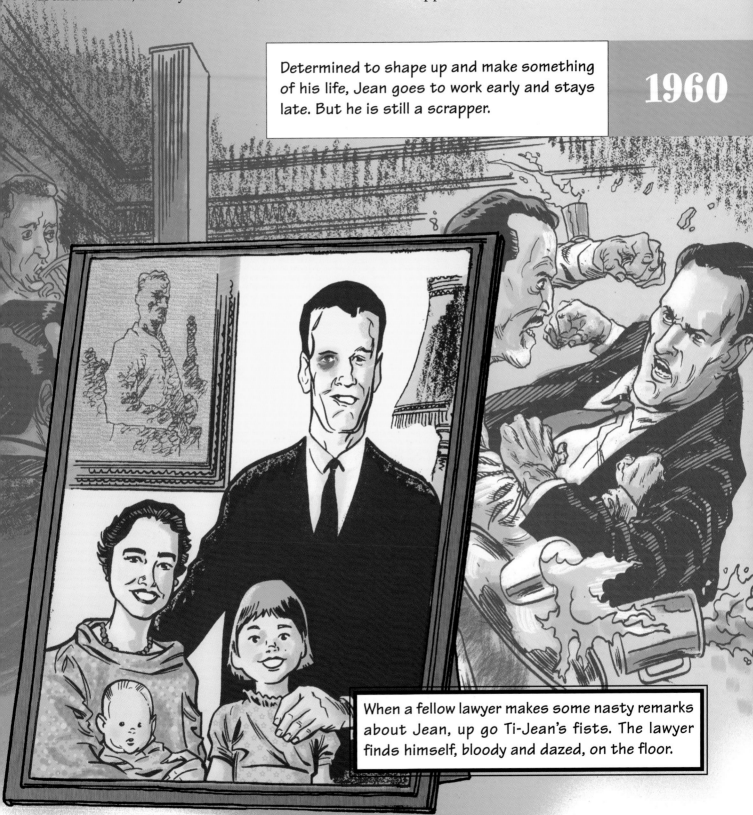

Determined to shape up and make something of his life, Jean goes to work early and stays late. But he is still a scrapper.

1960

When a fellow lawyer makes some nasty remarks about Jean, up go Ti-Jean's fists. The lawyer finds himself, bloody and dazed, on the floor.

1963

Now a Liberal, Jean decides to run against Gérard Lamy, a popular local politician.

"If it was a question of kids, my dad should be prime minister because he and my mom had 19 kids!"

Since Jean's political opponent keeps stressing the fact that he has 15 kids, Jean doesn't miss a chance to poke fun at him in public.

The little guy goes to Ottawa

In 1963, when a federal election was called, Jean decided to run for the Liberals. To everyone's amazement, he won the Liberal nomination for St-Maurice-Laflèche. This meant that he'd have to beat the local MP, Gérard Lamy, a member of the **Social Credit party**, in the general election.

Casino politics

Jean had very little cash to invest in the campaign, so his family and his supporters pooled their resources and canvassed their neighbours for money. Noticing that many people felt Jean didn't stand a chance of winning, his supporters devised a unique method of fundraising: they set up a pool and collected money from anyone who wanted to bet against a Jean victory!

Also during this period, when Jean gave a speech at a political rally hosted by Liberal leader **Lester B. Pearson**, one of his supporters held up a sign that said "Jean Chrétien: Our Future Prime Minister!" Pearson thought this was very funny. Little did he know!

1963
A federal election is called. Jean wins the Liberal nomination and, shortly after, the election.

1967
Jean becomes the youngest cabinet minister of the 20th century.

1968
Prime Minister Lester B. Pearson makes Jean minister of national revenue.

Pearson retires and Pierre Trudeau takes over as prime minister. He makes Jean minister of Indian affairs and northern development.

1974
Jean becomes president of the Treasury Board.

1979
Trudeau's Liberals are defeated in the federal election. Joe Clark becomes prime minister.

1980
The Quebec referendum is held. The separatists are defeated.

1986
Jean retires from politics.

1990
Jean returns to politics to become party leader.

1993
Prime Minister Brian Mulroney steps down. Kim Campbell takes over.

Baked-bean dinners and lots of slang

Jean worked hard on the campaign. He didn't have much money so he and Aline hosted baked-bean dinners, where he developed his populist style. "Populism" means "for the people," and Chrétien, with his crooked mouth, rough voice, and less-than-perfect pronunciation, wanted to come across as an ordinary working guy concerned with the problems of the average voter. He deliberately used plenty of slang and kept his speeches short and simple.

Jean's biggest problem was that he barely spoke English. He was having trouble reaching the English-speaking, or Anglophone, voters. Jean didn't let that stop him. He used humour to turn the situation to his advantage.

In April 1963, Jean beat his opponent. He was now an MP. His only disappointment was that his mother wasn't there for his victory.

Once on **Parliament Hill**, Jean was determined to improve his language skills. He read English magazines and made friends with Anglophone MPs, whom he asked to speak to him in English. "Ottawa was a very English town," he later wrote. "Very little French was spoken, except by security guards, waitresses, and maintenance men."

The Quiet Revolution

Back in Quebec, a "**Quiet Revolution**" was taking place. Quebecers were becoming convinced that corrupt governments and a repressive Catholic Church had kept them in poverty and ignorance for many generations. Things were now changing very rapidly. Quebecers wanted more say in how their province was governed.

As part of this change, **separatists** were trying to convince Francophones to break off from Canada and form their own country. They claimed this was necessary if Quebecers were to keep their language and culture. For some separatists, the battle was not so quiet. An extremist group called the FLQ (Front de libération du Québec) was planting bombs in mailboxes throughout Quebec. They even kidnapped two prominent politicians and held them for ransom. When that did not work, they killed one of their hostages. This greatly shocked the average Quebecer.

Jean vigorously disagreed with the FLQ. He wanted to keep Canada united and hated the use of violence to promote separatism. He thought that Quebecers would be much better off in a "full partnership" with Canada.

While waging his battle against separatism, Jean rose quickly through the ranks of the Liberal party. Starting off as Prime Minister Pearson's parliamentary secretary (assistant), he then became the same to the minister of

Most revolutions involve people fighting over territories or boundaries. Quebec's revolution was different. It was called "quiet" because it mostly involved a change in people's attitudes.

The revolution that was quiet

If you were French-speaking and grew up in Quebec in the 1950s, there was a good chance that your life was pretty much the same as if you had grown up in the 1850s.

Yes, you did have electricity, radio, and television, but many other things had not changed at all. English-speaking people ran all the big businesses and had all the really good jobs. The Catholic Church kept a close eye on what you did in your private life. It controlled nearly all the schools, teaching what the priests and nuns thought appropriate. It even stopped you from reading certain books.

Meanwhile, the Church's main ally, the Quebec government, made sure that the old ways and traditions were upheld, even if that meant most of its French-speaking citizens were kept poor and ignorant. **Maurice Duplessis**, leader of the **Union Nationale** party (and a symbol of this old style of leadership) was Quebec premier for nearly 20 years, starting in the 1930s.

He ruled the province with an iron grip and did everything to keep himself in power and keep Quebecers in their place. He even opposed giving women the vote, insisting that their only place was to remain at home and have as many children as possible.

In 1949, 5,000 miners went on strike in Asbestos and Thetford Mines. They wanted a salary increase of 15¢ an hour and asked for more protection from the dangerous dust. Duplessis responded to the strike by sending in the police to brutally attack the miners and crush their union. When Duplessis died in 1959, many Quebecers felt they now had a chance to put an end to an old and corrupt system, and bring Quebec into the 20th century at last.

The following year, the Liberal party, led by Jean Lesage, won the provincial elections. It wasted no time bringing in reforms. The Quebec government created a new department of education. This meant that the Church did not run schools anymore. Meanwhile, big building projects (like Expo '67 and gigantic hydroelectric dams) were started. A whole new feeling of hope and confidence was sweeping the province and there was talk of being *maîtres chez nous*, which means "masters in our own house."

But the Quiet Revolution was not just about politics. Artists, writers, and performers were also changing the way Quebecers felt about their past and their future. French-speaking Canadians were rising up and refusing to be held down by the Catholic Church or by big English-run businesses. People were taking pride in being French-Canadian and wanted to figure out how they could get along better with the rest of Canada. For some, the answer was separation and becoming their own country. But for Jean Chrétien, Pierre Trudeau, and others, the path for Quebec was to improve Canada for everyone.

The debate still goes on today.

For more information about Quebec's Quiet Revolution, visit our website at www.jackfruitpress.com.

finance. In 1967, when he joined the cabinet, he was, at 33, the youngest cabinet minister of the 20th century.

Although he was very busy, Jean didn't neglect his family during his rapid rise to power. After being appointed to the cabinet, he and Aline took their two children on a train ride across Canada. He was blown away by the splendour of the Rockies and by the friendliness of the people that they met. The trip made Jean more determined than ever to keep Canada together.

In early 1968, Prime Minister Pearson made Jean the minister of national revenue. Soon after, Pearson retired and **Pierre Trudeau** replaced him as prime minister. Trudeau called an election only days after becoming PM. Because Trudeau was very popular, the Liberals won a smashing majority.

A month later, Prime Minister Trudeau appointed Jean minister of Indian affairs and northern development. The appointment came as a surprise. Jean knew nothing about aboriginal issues. Trudeau said that was why he was chosen—Jean would think of new ways to run things.

Once he was at Indian Affairs, Jean discovered that **First Nations peoples** had many legitimate grievances against the Canadian government. He thought it was unfair that aboriginals were confined to poverty-stricken reserves and generally kept out of Canadian society. He wanted to abolish the reserves, but First Nations people (and some others) were afraid that this would be the end of their unique culture. Jean was forced to shelve this plan. He had more luck with the northern development part of his job. He established 10 new national parks, an achievement he was extremely proud of.

Butchering the anthem

One of Jean's less proud moments happened during a tour of the North-west Territories in 1970. He was escorting **Queen Elizabeth II** and her family around and the trip was going well. In Fort Providence, Jean and the president of the Historic Sites and Monuments Board were scheduled to unveil a plaque. A huge crowd had gathered for the event. The president was supposed to lead the crowd in singing "O Canada" but, at the last minute, confessed to Jean that he had a lousy voice and was terrified to sing in public.

Jean offered to lead the singing himself. After a few bars in his gravelly, tuneless voice, Jean realized that no one was joining in. He knew only the French version, while the Queen and the audience knew only the English version. Jean slogged on, butchering the anthem, while the Queen and the crowd squirmed. Aline later described this as the most embarrassing moment of her life.

From one job to the next, Jean climbed toward the job he really wanted— prime minister.

One of Jean's most awkward moments happens during a tour of the North. He's escorting Queen Elizabeth II to the unveiling of a plaque in Fort Providence, Northwest Territories. A huge crowd has gathered for the event.

O Canada, terre de nos aïeux!

Jean leads the crowd in singing "O Canada"—in French. The Queen and the audience know only the English version. After a few bars in his gravelly, tuneless voice, Jean realizes that no one is joining in. He slogs on, butchering the anthem. Meanwhile the Queen waits, his wife Aline squirms, and the crowd wonders.

Quebec has always argued that it needs special powers to protect and promote its culture.

When the Parti Québécois won the 1976 election with a large majority, the issue of Quebec independence became a hot topic.

In 1980, René Lévesque, the PQ's popular leader, called a referendum that asked voters whether Quebec should become a sovereign state.

The PQ said that an independent Quebec would keep a special association with Canada, but would make its own laws, collect its own taxes, and so on.

The "yes" side got about 40 per cent of the vote, and the "no" side got about 60.

Dr. No

In 1974, Prime Minister Trudeau made Jean president of the Treasury Board. Jean now had to decide how much money each government department would get. Jean loved this position. He wrote, "Let the philosophers philosophize elsewhere.... I want to be where the cash is."

He ran a tight ship. He turned down so many funding proposals that he became known as "Dr. No."

Jean then became minister of industry, trade, and commerce, then finally landed the job he really wanted: he became the first French-Canadian finance minister. But inflation was up and business was down. Voters were fed up with the Liberals and they elected the Conservatives.

In June 1979, **Progressive Conservative party** leader **Joe Clark** replaced Trudeau as prime minister. However, Prime Minister Clark was only able to stay in power for seven months. The PCs lost a **non-confidence vote** (they got outvoted on a major piece of legislation) and had to call a new election. Pierre Trudeau led the Liberals to another big win. Jean was re-elected in his home riding for the seventh time in a row.

Jean's main task was to prevent Canada from splitting in two. The **Quebec referendum**—a vote in which the people of Quebec would decide if they wanted their province to separate from Canada—was scheduled for May 20, 1980. Jean travelled around Quebec, speaking from the heart about the beauty of Canada, encouraging people to vote against separation. Thanks, in part, to him, the separatists were defeated in the referendum.

Bringing home the Charter

Jean was soon handed a new assignment. Trudeau was determined to bring home the **British North America Act**, Canada's constitution. Oddly enough, although the BNA Act defined Canada's constitution, it was still in British hands because Ottawa and the provinces had never agreed on an amending formula (a way of reforming the constitution). Jean met with provincial officials to hammer out an amending formula and a **Charter of Rights and Freedoms**. In the middle of all this, Wellie died at the age of 92. Jean was devastated but could not afford much time to mourn. A year and a half later, after much debate in both the Canadian and British parliaments, the Canadian Constitution, including the new Charter of Rights and Freedoms, was brought home to Canada. It was a very important moment for the country.

Shortly after repatriating Canada's constitution, Prime Minister Trudeau decided that he'd had enough of politics. He announced that he would step down as Liberal party leader. Jean figured he had a fair shot at being chosen as the new leader. He had experience and was a proven winner.

In a matter of a few short years, the little guy from Shawinigan manages to accumulate a truly impressive list of accomplishments.

RESUMÉ

1958
Called to the QUEBEC BAR

1962-63
Becomes director of the BAR of TROIS-RIVIÈRES

1963
Elected as Liberal MP in St-Maurice-Laflèche

1965
Named parliamentary secretary to Prime Minister LESTER PEARSON

inister of
Indian
Affairs

$$$

1990
Elected as leader of Liberal party replacing JOHN TURNER

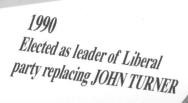

The **Grits** (a nickname for the Liberal party), however, had other ideas. In their tradition of alternating between French and English leaders, they chose **John Turner** instead.

The party's decision was a bitter pill for Jean to swallow, but he agreed to stay on as deputy prime minister and minister of external affairs. The Liberals under Turner were slaughtered in the next election and the Conservatives, led by **Brian Mulroney**, took over.

Speaking straight from the heart

It was at this time that Jean wrote his autobiography. It was called *Straight from the Heart*, and it sold like hotcakes. Shortly afterwards, Jean and John Turner had a disagreement and so, in 1986, Jean left politics to work as a lawyer once again. In the spring of 1990, Turner stepped down as party leader and Jean tried his chance at the leadership of the party. He won easily on the first ballot of the party convention, beating **Paul Martin**. Le petit gars de Shawinigan had finally triumphed. He was leader of the Liberal party.

Jean had no interest in being Opposition leader. While he was waiting to become prime minister, the Liberal **spin doctors** decided to clean up Ti-Jean, working to improve his speech, hair, and teeth. They sent him to speech coaches who made him read from prepared texts, something he'd never done before. Problem was, Jean now sounded like a robot as he read his speeches, desperately trying to say his vowels clearly, self-conscious in a way he had never been before. Aline and his close supporters were not impressed. They realized that Jean's appeal lay in the fact that he was a plain-spoken guy who sounded funny but spoke from the heart. Jean took their advice, ditched the prepared notes and speech coaches, and went back to his old rip-'em-up speaking style. While audiences often had problems understanding what Jean was saying, they loved his simple, unpolished, populist style.

When Prime Minister Mulroney resigned in 1993, **Kim Campbell** was chosen as his successor. The Conservatives were desperate because they knew that they were now very unpopular with the voters. They tried to undermine the Liberals by running a TV ad that emphasized Jean's crooked mouth and asked, "Does this man look like a prime minister?" The public hated the ad, and hated the **Tories** (a nickname for the Conservative party) even more for airing it. Jean's response was gracious: "It's true that I have a physical defect," he said. "When I was a kid, people were laughing at me. But I accepted that because God gave me other qualities and I am grateful."

Talk about an extreme makeover that really bombed!

Jean's English was pretty bad, but he sounded much worse when spin doctors tried to remake his image.

What was the secret of Jean Chrétien's popularity?

Many careers (like that of a film director or school principal) can be difficult because they involve making decisions that affect a lot of other people. Being the prime minister is one of those careers. You have to convince millions of people that you're the right person to run Canada. To do this well, you have to develop your own leadership style—a way of telling others what you think should be done and getting them to believe in you.

There are all sorts of ways you can do this, and our different prime ministers have had many different leadership styles. For instance, Pierre Trudeau was often thought of as an "elitist" (a person who thought he was better than others). He had little patience for those who could not understand him, or anyone he felt was wrong. At times, Pierre could be arrogant and even rude. But this style of leadership worked well for him because it convinced others that he really believed in what he said and did, and that he'd never back down from his own principles.

Brian Mulroney was a different type of leader. Before becoming a politician, Mulroney had been a businessperson, and he'd learned to be charming and smooth as a way of getting other people to trust him. Some people called his way a "presidential style" because he came across as an important person who could be comfortable hobnobbing with the rich and famous.

Jean Chrétien had his own leadership style, which people called "populist." This was because he talked and acted as if he were just an ordinary guy doing an ordinary job. He also made it clear that he did not like to be with people who thought they were better than others; Jean thought they were snobs.

Another feature of Jean's leadership style was that he talked in a simple way. He hardly ever used big words and often included slang terms in his speeches. Not everyone liked his style of speaking. They felt he often embarrassed the country when he talked with other world leaders. But many ordinary Canadians thought Jean was talking from his heart. They liked the fact that he could make them understand where he stood on an issue without having to ramble on for hours.

Sometimes, though, Jean was less than completely honest about being an ordinary guy. He once answered a question by saying, "Well, I am not a lawyer." This comment made him sound friendly and uncomplicated. It also made for a good "sound bite" (a short sentence that is often used in news headlines). There was just one little problem: it wasn't true! Jean was trained as a lawyer and worked as one for many years. Some people thought Jean's populist style was more of an act than a reality. They pointed out that his daughter was married to one of the richest men in Canada and that Jean himself had become a millionaire.

Even though he was rich, Jean never acted like a snob, and, for millions of Canadians, he was a real person they could trust. Quite a few might have disagreed with his ideas, but they still identified with him and believed he was telling the truth when he spoke to them.

For more information about leadership styles, visit our website at www.jackfruitpress.com.

With a second referendum coming up, Québécois politicians Lucien Bouchard and Jacques Parizeau rush around the province, stirring people up with powerful speeches in favour of separation.

At first, Jean stayed out of the referendum battle at the request of the premier of Quebec. But as the referendum deadline loomed, Jean decided to step into the fray. There was only one week left.

Taking charge of the country

1993
Kim Campbell becomes Canada's first female prime minister. She holds the title for just over four months.

1993
Jean becomes Canada's 20th prime minister.

1994
The North Atlantic Free Trade Agreement between Canada, Mexico, and the United States comes into effect.

1995
A second referendum is held in Quebec. Once again, the separatists lose—but just barely.

1996
Jean grabs a heckler by the neck and pushes him to the ground. The incident makes national front-page news.

Major floods cause damage in the Saguenay area of Quebec.

On November 4, 1993, Chrétien was installed as Canada's 20th prime minister. While he was thrilled that the Liberals had won a huge majority, he now had to deal with some hard realities. The country was in bad shape financially. The economy was sluggish, unemployment was high, and the debt and deficit kept getting bigger. By 1993, Canada's yearly deficit had hit $41 billion while the country's overall debt was pushing $500 billion.

This was not a good situation, so Chrétien turned to Paul Martin, who was known to be adept with numbers and cash. He appointed Martin as his finance minister. Martin took one look at Canada's bank account and freaked out. The situation was so bad, he was afraid that foreign banks might stop lending the government money or, worse, demand instant payment for cash owed.

Chrétien liked spending money as much as any other Liberal, but he realized that a financial reckoning was in order. So, on February 27, 1995, Mar-

Results of the 1993 election:

Jean Chrétien becomes
Canada's 20th prime minister

Population:	27,296,859
Eligible voters:	19,906,796
Valid votes cast:	13,667,671

How the numbers stacked up:

Party	# votes	# seats
PC	2,186,422	2
Liberal	5,647,952	177
NDP	939,575	9
Reform	2,559,245	52
BQ	1,846,024	54
Other	488,453	1
Total	13,667,671	295

Issues: economic recession
constitutional reform

tin announced huge spending cuts: the biggest federal government spending cuts ever. The Liberals slashed $25 billion in spending over three years and cut 45,000 government jobs.

The provinces were upset because Chrétien slashed $7 billion from the Canada Health and Social Transfer (money that Ottawa gave the provinces to spend on health, education, and welfare). As a result, provinces were forced to give less money to universities, cut welfare payments, and close hospitals.

Realizing that such cuts would be very unpopular with Canadians, Chrétien went on CBC radio to defend his budget. "It's painful," he said. "But it's needed."

Thanks to these drastic cuts to public services, the Liberals found that they could get by with less cash. Canada didn't go broke. The federal deficit was eliminated over several years and the national debt went down.

A second referendum

Soon, Chrétien had more pressing concerns than money matters and government spending. In Quebec, a newly re-elected Parti Québécois government was preparing a second referendum on independence. This situation was far from new for Jean. He had seen it all before when Prime Minister Trudeau was in power. At that time, the separatists had challenged Canadian unity by inviting Quebecers to vote in a referendum on independence. Thanks mostly to Pierre Trudeau's deft handling of the situation, Quebec had decided to stay in Canada.

This new referendum was promising more of the same, and yet it was also quite different. The separatist movement had been changing over the 1980s and '90s. It had been redefining itself to become more attractive to Quebecers. Many Quebecers had been afraid of separation because they thought it would cause them great financial hardship if Quebec became an independent country. As a result, the independence movement had changed. Instead of referring to themselves as "separatists," they said they were "sovereignists." They explained that they simply wanted more autonomy for Quebec—that is, they wanted to stay part of Canada but have more freedom to make laws that protected French language and culture. This new spin on the old separation argument made it much more likely that a greater number of Quebecers would vote in favour of a new relationship with Canada.

Debt, deficit, and sometimes a surplus

Canada's debt and deficit were on everyone's minds in the early 1990s. As prime minister, Jean was very much concerned with this situation. He dearly wanted to improve the country's financial standing.

To get a better picture of Canada's situation at the time, think about your allowance. Suppose your parents give you a few dollars each week. If in a week you receive more money than you spend, you have a surplus for the week—extra money available to spend on something else. If, however, you spend more than you received during the week, you have a deficit—you have to get the extra money you spent from somewhere. If you have no savings to take it from, you'll need to borrow it from someone. The total amount of money you owe is called your debt. The finances of a country work the same way. If the government spends more in a year than it collects, it has a deficit for that year. Unless there was a surplus saved up from earlier years, the country will have to borrow. The total amount of money that the country owes is its debt, which equals the sum of all its deficits over the years (minus any surpluses it uses to pay off what it owes).

By 1993, Canada had a yearly deficit of $41 billion (the country was spending $41 billion more than it was taking in each year) and the country's overall debt (the sum of all the previous yearly deficits) was almost $500 billion, or half a trillion dollars! Many people were afraid that Canada would go broke.

Sometimes people wonder why a government doesn't simply print more money when it needs some, but this would actually make things worse. A flood of new money causes massive inflation (prices rise while the value of the country's money remains the same or decreases). This happened in Germany after World War I. Germany had no money, so the government printed more. The money quickly lost its value. It became so worthless that people had to fill wheelbarrows with bills just to buy their groceries.

Canada preferred to get its money from the banks. However, if a country's deficit grows too large, banks might refuse to lend it money. Even worse, they can demand repayment on all of the country's debt right away.

Let's go back to your allowance. Imagine what would happen if you were deeply in debt and your parents stopped paying you any allowance. With no money coming in, you'd go broke very quickly. And the people you owed money to would be really, really angry.

Jean Chrétien didn't want the country to go broke, so he had Minister of Finance Paul Martin make big cuts in government spending. Over time, the Liberals managed to turn the yearly deficit into a surplus so they could start paying down the country's debt.

For more information about debt and deficit, visit our website at www.jackfruitpress.com.

Jean leaps into action

The second referendum was to be held on October 30, 1995. Jacques Parizeau, leader of the Parti Québécois, was now getting help from **Lucien Bouchard**. A former federal member of Parliament, Bouchard had switched allegiance and was now rushing around Quebec, stirring the people up with powerful speeches in favour of what he called "a sovereign association with Canada." Jean kept silent at first, but finally leapt into action. He met with his ministers at an emotional meeting in late October. The referendum vote was only five days away. He accused Bouchard and Parizeau of getting away with lies and more lies. He described the weekend he had just spent at the **United Nations** with leader after leader telling him that they couldn't understand what Quebec was doing. His voice broke and his eyes filled with tears. His ministers watched in stunned silence as the tough guy, who used to settle disagreements with his fists, broke down in front of them.

At the very last minute, the federal government scheduled a huge rally in Montreal. About 150,000 people showed up from different parts of the country. Jean addressed the crowd with a simple, heartfelt speech. "When I see you all, coming from the provinces in Canada and from all parts of Quebec, I have never felt as proud…to be a Quebecer and as proud to be Canadian. *Vive le Québec! Vive le Canada!* …We will make the changes that are needed…[so that] Canada will move into the 21st century united from sea to sea."

Two-fisted Ti-Jean

The vote was extremely close but Quebecers decided to stay in Canada. Jean sensed that Canada had come close to losing Quebec and that he had escaped political disaster by the skin of his teeth. He was not in a good mood. A few months later, looking like a gangster in black coat and sunglasses, he made his way through a crowd celebrating Flag Day near Parliament Hill. When a protester heckled him, Ti-Jean grabbed him around the neck and pushed him to the ground. TV cameras caught the whole thing on tape. "He was right in front of me, shouting and trying to block my way, so I took him out. He was a lightweight, probably. I just moved him out," the unapologetic PM told reporters. The incident was front-page news across Canada. Some members of the public liked the PM's tough-guy moves. Others didn't. Many mocked Jean for his poor "anger management techniques." Fortunately for Jean, the protester didn't press charges.

To avoid another referendum like the one in 1995, where unclear language was used to confuse voters, Jean's government passed the Clarity Act.

This act laid out the rules by which a province can separate from Canada.

It says that a separation referendum has to be based on a clearly worded question, and that one side or the other must win by an obvious majority.

Who decides what's clear and obvious? The House of Commons!

Jean and Aline already have two children, France and Hubert, but they want to expand their family. The Chrétiens decide to adopt a baby.

Partly because of Jean's experience as minister of Indian affairs, the Chrétiens adopt a First Nations child.

Personal sorrows and triumphs

In the late 1960s, Jean and Aline already had two children, France and Hubert, but wanted to expand their family. Doctors had advised Aline not to have another child, so the Chrétiens decided to adopt a child. Partly because Jean was minister of Indian affairs at the time, they chose to adopt a First Nations child.

A healthy child

Jean's brother, Michel, who was working as a doctor in Inuvik, went to the local orphanage to scout out three kids who were available for adoption. Jean and Aline couldn't bring themselves to select one, so Michel picked out an 18-month-old boy. He was a healthy child but there wasn't much information about his birth parents.

The Chrétiens were delighted and named the boy Michel. The whole family showered Michel with love but it was soon obvious that there was something wrong. He didn't respond when his parents tried to talk to him or play with him, and he was often withdrawn and silent. When he started school, he skipped classes and got terrible marks. Jean did what his father, Wellie, had done. He sent Michel to a series of boarding schools, hoping that they might settle him down. Michel continued to have problems, however, and Jean, unlike Wellie, found it impossible to discipline his son.

1969
Jean and Aline's soon-to-be-adopted son, Michel, is born.

1971
Jean's brother visits an Inuvik orphanage to find a child to adopt.

Jean and Aline adopt 18-month-old Michel.

1972
It becomes obvious that something is wrong with Michel.

1980s
Michel does poorly in school, skips classes, drinks heavily, and sometimes runs away from home.

He is sent off to boarding school in the hope that it will help him.

1990
Michel is arrested.

1992
Michel stands trial and is sentenced to three years in prison.

1995
Aline confronts a knife-wielding stranger at 24 Sussex Drive.

2002
Michel is arrested again.

Fetal Alcohol Syndrome

When he became a teenager, Michel started drinking heavily and sometimes ran away from home. Jean and Aline took Michel to doctors, counsellors, and therapists, but nothing worked. As frustrated as they were, they never complained about Michel's behaviour. In 1990, the police arrested Michel for breaking the law. He went on trial in 1992 and Jean, who was then Opposition leader, spent his mornings in Montreal, attending Michel's court sessions before going back to Ottawa for **question period**, then returning to Montreal for the evening. Jean refused to talk about Michel's trial with reporters. He didn't look for sympathy, even when Michel was found guilty and sentenced to three years in jail. It appeared that Michel suffered from **Fetal Alcohol Syndrome**, a condition that affects children whose mothers drink too much alcohol during pregnancy.

Influential new relations

Although Hubert had dyslexia and asthma and had some trouble in school, he and France had good childhoods. France eventually married André Desmarais, whose father ran Power Corporation. The Chrétiens were now related to some of the richest and most influential business people in Canada. Populist Ti-Jean found this highly amusing.

Jean and Aline remained extremely close, a tightly knit couple who leaned on each other for strength. Jean said that he not only might not have become a leader without Aline, he might not have even finished school.

Aline saves Jean's life

One night, at 3:00 a.m., Aline thought she heard footsteps in the hallway outside the Chrétiens' bedroom in **24 Sussex Drive**, the prime minister's official residence. When she got out of bed and walked into the hallway, she came face to face with a stranger who had a jackknife in his hand.

Aline slammed the bedroom door shut, locked it, woke up Jean, and called the police. Jean grabbed an Inuit stone carving for self-defence. The Mounties came quickly to the rescue, seized the intruder, and arrested him. The man turned out to be a hard-line separatist. He told police he expected to be made a hero in Quebec for killing the PM.

The incident was downplayed by the Mounties and the media until Jean gave a news conference to let Canadians know how serious it had actually been. The intruder had planned to cut Jean's throat open with a knife.

Speaking of Power Corporation, another prime minister worked there before he got into politics. Who do you think that is? (Hint: he became PM after Jean retired.)

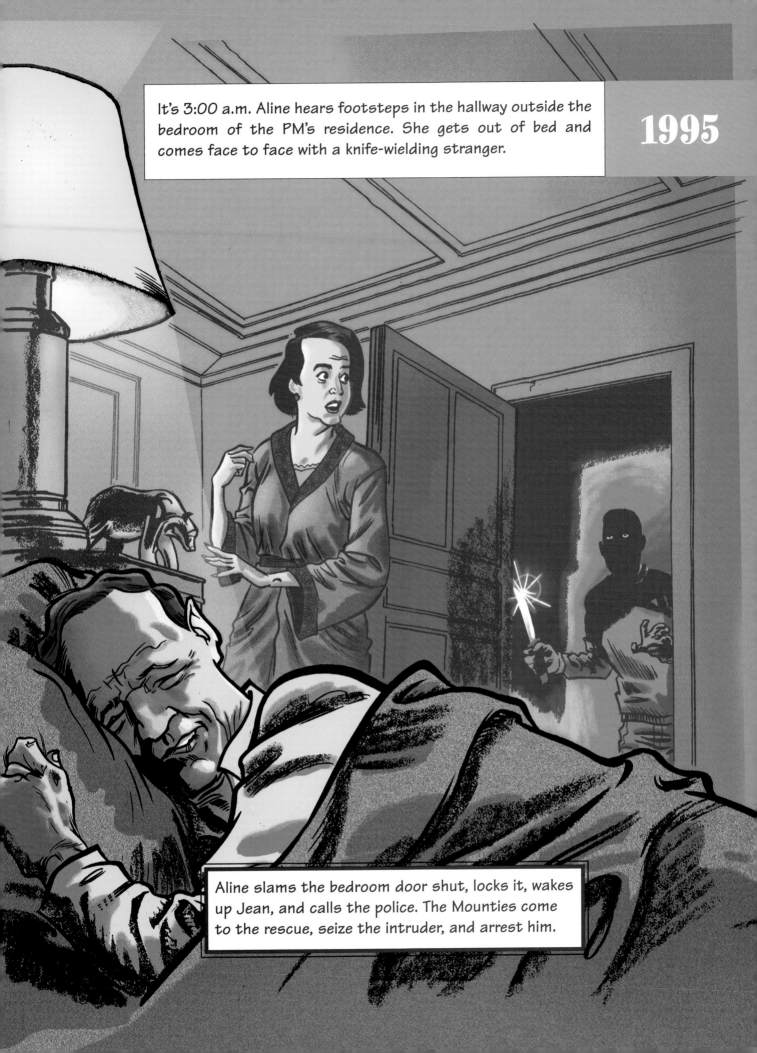

2000

The economy is humming along and the government now has a budget surplus of $12 billion. Behind the scenes, though, some Liberals start a campaign to get rid of Jean.

Opponents say Jean is wishy-washy. Many people don't like his tight-fisted financial policies. His deafness and his struggles with speaking English sometimes lead to misunderstandings. In spite of it all, Jean's Liberals win election after election.

Driven, wishy-washy, and a has-been?

When he became prime minister, the once unruly Ti-Jean kept a precise schedule. His cabinet meetings always started at 10:00 a.m. sharp on Tuesday mornings and ended exactly at noon. His meetings were so speedy that the entire agenda was often covered ahead of schedule. He would instruct his cabinet members to come up with issues to discuss so that cabinet didn't come out early and give the media the impression they were slacking.

Jean also made it home for lunch as often as possible. As well as running up and down the steps in the House of Commons, he took a brisk walk each day. If he didn't stretch his legs, he would get so jumpy he couldn't sit still. Sound familiar? Like his father before him, he worked non-stop, although he occasionally played golf. In the evenings, he read policy papers and government notes. It was hard for him to take long vacations because he found it almost impossible to relax.

Wishy-washy

As prime minister, Jean Chrétien had a core set of values that guided his actions and the policies of his government. He wanted to keep Canada united, provide social programs to help the disadvantaged, and regulate the economy. He tended to be cautious when it came to launching new government programs. Supporters said he was just being practical. Opponents said he was being wishy-washy.

1997
The Liberals win another majority government under Jean's leadership.

The Calgary Declaration—a constitutional reform—is accepted by all provincial and territorial leaders but Quebec's.

1998
Jean makes an official visit to Cuba.

The Supreme Court rules that Quebec can't legally separate from Canada without prior negotiations with the federal and provincial governments.

1999
Canada takes a seat on the United Nations Security Council.

Nunavut becomes Canada's third territory.

The first Canadian boards the International Space Station.

The world's population surpasses six billion.

2000
Jean receives an honourary doctorate from Memorial University in St. John's, Newfoundland.

Former prime minister Pierre Trudeau dies.

For example, Jean promised in the 1993 election to get rid of the Goods and Services Tax (GST), a sales tax that added 7 per cent to all the things Canadians bought. Jean knew that everyone hated the GST. He tried to come up with a new tax that would be collected by the federal and provincial governments. Unable to reach an agreement with all the provinces, Jean was forced to give up on the scheme. Realizing that the government needed every tax dollar it could lay its hands on, Jean decided to keep the GST, in spite of the public's howls of protest. Some members of his own party were also appalled because they felt that he should have kept this promise.

No big promises

In the June 1997 election, the Liberals deliberately avoided making any big promises. Instead, they boasted about how they had successfully lowered inflation and the deficit. And, they said, they would continue to do the same. They won another majority.

Jean's public statements could be as vague as his policies. Sometimes reporters scratched their heads, trying to figure out what the prime minister really meant, or even exactly what he'd said. The PM's deafness and his struggles with speaking English sometimes led to misunderstandings. Once, in a press conference with US president **Bill Clinton**, a reporter asked Chrétien his opinion about illegal drugs flooding into the United States from Canada. He thought for a moment, then said, "It's more trade." The press laughed. Bill rephrased the question for Jean's benefit. "Oh, drugs!" said Jean. "I heard [you say] 'trucks.'"

During his first two terms as PM, Jean appointed several talented women to high office. **Sheila Copps** became the first female deputy prime minister, **Anne McLellan** became justice minister, and **Adrienne Clarkson** was named **governor general**, the first visible minority to occupy the position. He also made **Beverley McLachlin** the first woman chief justice of the **Supreme Court of Canada**.

A whispering campaign

By mid-2000, the economy was humming along and the Liberals were enjoying a budget surplus of about $12 billion. They had not only gotten rid of the deficit, they could now pay off a big chunk of the national debt.

The hottest issue on Parliament Hill was the whispering campaign by some Liberals to get rid of Jean. They wanted Minister of Finance Paul Martin to be the new PM. Jean chose to ignore these voices of opposition within his own party.

Back in the House of Commons, the leader of the new Canadian Alliance party dared Jean to call an election or resign. Jean did just that, and set the election date for November 2000.

During the 1993 election, Sheila Copps promised to resign her seat if the GST weren't scrapped.

It wasn't, and she was forced to keep her word.

But in the next by-election she ran for office again and won her seat back!

Jean's deafness and his struggles with English sometimes lead to misunderstandings. The PM's public statements often leave reporters wondering what he meant.

Oh, "drugs" ... I heard "trucks"!

In a press conference with US president Bill Clinton, a reporter asks Chrétien his opinion about illegal drugs flooding into the United States from Canada. Jean says, "It's more trade." The press laughs. Bill rephrases the question for Jean's benefit.

2001

On September 11, terrorists crash hijacked planes into the World Trade Center in New York City and the Pentagon in Washington, DC. Though shocked, Jean doesn't lose his cool.

Against the recommendations of some advisers, Jean refuses to order government workers home for the day. He calculates that such an action might cause Canadians to think Canada is also under attack and lead to panic. He also deliberately avoids addressing the nation on TV.

Final power struggles

The most interesting issue of the 2000 election was the feud between Jean and Paul Martin. The power struggle between the two men had become public knowledge. Conservative Joe Clark accused Jean of calling an election just to prevent Martin from taking his job, and Jean had a tough time denying the charge. Others thought Jean was becoming paranoid about threats to his leadership. They accused him of holding on to too much power and gleefully squashing those who didn't agree with him.

But in spite of their internal struggles, the Liberals steamrolled over the opposition and won their third straight majority government. Some critics wondered if they would ever be defeated.

Response to 9/11

On **September 11, 2001**, when terrorists crashed hijacked planes into the World Trade Center in New York City, Jean was horrified but didn't lose his cool. Against the recommendations of some advisers, he refused to order government workers home for the day because he feared such an action might cause Canadians to think they were also under attack and lead to panic. He didn't address the nation on TV, although he

2000
The Liberals win a third majority government in a federal election. This has never been done before.

2001
Terrorists attack the World Trade Center in New York and the Pentagon in Washington, DC, killing an estimated 3,000 people.

American, British, Australian, and Canadian troops invade Afghanistan.

Canada becomes the first country in the world to legalize medicinal marijuana.

2002
Canada signs the Kyoto Protocol to reduce greenhouse gases.

2003
Jean resigns as PM.

Paul Martin becomes Canada's 21st prime minister.

The Iraq war begins.

2004
Jean returns to practising law.

Testimony begins at the Gomery Commission's inquiry into the sponsorship scandal.

2005
Jean testifies at the Gomery inquiry.

39

expressed his sorrow to the US ambassador. A few days later, he also arranged an outdoor memorial service on Parliament Hill for the victims of the terrorist attack, and 100,000 people attended. They sang the US national anthem and mourned the dead. In his speech, Jean directed these words to Americans through their ambassador to Canada: "Do not despair. You are not alone. We are with you. The whole world is with you. The great **Martin Luther King**, in describing times of trial and tribulation, once said that 'In the end, it is not the words of your enemies that you remember, it is the silence of your friends.' Mr. Ambassador, as your fellow Americans grieve and rebuild, there will be no silence from Canada. Our friendship has no limit."

Growing cries of scandal

The last few months of Jean's time as prime minister were marred by charges of corruption. A report by Canada's **auditor general** indicated that millions of tax dollars had gone missing. The money had been spent on a federal government program that Jean had personally supported. The federal government had paid tens of millions of dollars to various Quebec advertising agencies (many of them supporters of the Liberals) for projects that never really happened. This state of affairs came to be known as the **sponsorship scandal**.

Organizers of cultural and sporting events had received massive amounts of cash from Ottawa in exchange for displaying Canadian flags, red maple leaves, and government logos at these events, which took place mainly in Quebec. Throughout 2001 and 2002, the media published a stream of stories about millions of dollars connected to this program being mislaid or not being properly accounted for.

Meanwhile, Jean's war with Paul Martin continued. Supporters of the two men bickered constantly, undermining each other and splintering the Liberal party. A frustrated Jean demanded that no one in his cabinet campaign for the Liberal leadership as long as he was still in charge. Martin refused to accept this demand.

What happened next is complicated. Jean's supporters said that Martin resigned from the cabinet and Martin's supporters said he was fired. In any case, once he was no longer in the cabinet, Martin concentrated his efforts on gaining support for his bid to become the next leader of the Liberal party.

A lasting legacy

In August 2002, Jean's supporters circulated a letter to Liberal MPs asking them to support his leadership. Signing it was seen as a test of loyalty. The letter outraged Liberals who thought Jean should be planning a dignified

Ever heard of the Gomery Commission? It was the group that Prime Minister Paul Martin called to investigate the sponsorship scandal.

It was named after the man who ran it— retired judge John Gomery.

Terrorism and September 11, 2001

Terrorists use violence to try to further their political, religious, or social causes. Unlike ordinary criminals, who attack individuals for money or personal power, terrorists care only about their cause and are willing to attack anyone, even innocent people. They are not concerned with the rules of war, which state clearly that it is illegal for soldiers to kill civilians. In the mind of a terrorist, even people who are totally unarmed and innocent deserve to die if they belong to the church, political party, or nation that the terrorists oppose.

One of the worst terrorist attacks of recent memory occurred on September 11, 2001 (usually referred to as "9/11"), when a group of radical Muslims hijacked a series of airplanes and deliberately crashed them into the World Trade Center in New York City and the Pentagon (headquarters of the US military) in Washington, DC. A fourth plane, probably headed for the White House, crashed in Pennsylvania, possibly because the passengers fought against the hijackers.

After the 9/11 attacks, airports were shut down in Canada and the United States. No planes were allowed to take off. Two hundred and twenty-four planes carrying 33,000 passengers that had been headed for the United States were diverted to Canada instead, most to Nova Scotia and Newfoundland. Canadians opened up their homes and hearts to these passengers, providing shelter, food, and comfort.

Prime Minister Chrétien, in a speech to the House of Commons on September 17, 2001, emphasized that terrorists attack the values of all people. "Let us be clear," he said about the destruction of the World Trade Center. "This was not just an attack on the United States. These cold-blooded killers struck a blow at the values and beliefs of free and civilized people everywhere."

The terrorists who committed the atrocities of 9/11 claimed to be devout Muslims. They explained that they were punishing the United States for interfering in the affairs of many Muslim countries around the world. They pointed out that decades of American interventions in these countries had created much despair and desperation, which eventually led many youths to rise up in protest. They also objected to the United States' strong support of Israel.

Most Muslims were horrified by the attacks and separated themselves from the extremists who had caused this event. They pointed out that Islam (another name for the Muslim faith) teaches peace and love, not war.

For more information about terrorism, visit our website at www.jackfruitpress.com.

exit from office instead of clinging to power. Barely half of the Liberal caucus signed the letter. Jean saw this as a devastating blow to his leadership and announced that he would not run in another election. He said he would step down in February 2004, at which time a successor could take his job. He denied that he was being hounded out of office.

Jean used his remaining few months in power to make a lasting legacy. He signed the Kyoto Protocol, an international agreement to limit air pollution and greenhouse gas emissions. Three months later, he turned down a request to help US president George Bush invade Iraq. Jean said he would provide combat troops only if the United Nations Security Council agreed to the invasion.

The United States was claiming that the leader of Iraq was a threat to the security of the world and should be overthrown. They even said that Iraq was hiding the terrorists who were responsible for the attacks on the Pentagon and the World Trade Center. The UN council didn't agree. They felt that the United States did not have enough proof to support these claims. As time passed and the war in Iraq dragged on, many Canadians came to appreciate the wisdom of Jean's decision. This grew even more evident when it became clear that Iraq did not have any weapons of mass destruction, as the US government had claimed.

Jean also dealt with other important issues in his last few months in office. He increased spending on health care and the military, and promised to introduce legislation to legalize marriages between people of the same sex. Realizing that same-sex marriage was a tricky subject for some Canadians, Jean said, "For someone of my generation . . . this is a very difficult issue. But I have learned . . . that society evolves and that the concept of human rights evolves more quickly than some of us might have predicted—and sometimes even in ways that make some people uncomfortable. But . . . we have to live up to our responsibilities."

Ti-Jean says goodbye

On November 6, 2003, Jean participated in his last question period as leader of the Liberal party. He received tributes from all parties in the House. A week later, the Liberals held a convention and elected Paul Martin as their new leader. Party members praised Ti-Jean and spoke glowingly of his accomplishments. A week after that, he announced that he would resign two months earlier than he'd planned, and on December 12, 2003, he handed his resignation to the governor general. He also resigned his seat in the House of Commons and went back to work as a lawyer.

Jean is proud of his Team Canada initiative. He is the first Canadian prime minister to travel around the world with groups of business professionals chosen to promote Canadian business.

1994

Jean takes advantage of a business trip to joke with reporters and business people with whom he is sharing a jet. The group is on its way to yet another Team Canada location.

Jean Chrétien: Smarts, grit

Jean Chrétien left a mixed legacy. On the one hand, he was Canada's "raging bull" prime minister. His squabbles with Paul Martin were seen as unprofessional and undignified. He could sometimes be mean to others and he rarely backed down from a fight.

People wondered if his handling of the GST showed that he cared more about power and money than he did about keeping his promises. And while he might not have been directly responsible for the sponsorship scandal, many people felt he should have prevented it from happening.

On the other hand, the story of le petit gars de Shawinigan is one of triumph, grit, and determination. He refused to be held back by a string of challenges that might have stopped someone less determined. Jean rose from humble beginnings and worked hard behind the scenes until he landed leadership positions.

Under Prime Minister Trudeau, he helped bring

Who could possibly forget Jean's performance at the Gomery Commission inquiry? Accused of having wasted public money on monogrammed golf balls, Jean showed up with a briefcase full of props. He then mockingly identified several balls in his

and dogged determination

home Canada's constitution. He created 10 new national parks and tried to get a better deal for aboriginal people. He fought against separatism, helping to ensure that Quebec stayed in Canada. He brought order to Canada's finances and opened high-level doors to women. He initiated legislation to legalize marriages between partners of the same sex, and kept Canada out of the war in Iraq.

Throughout his career, Jean never wavered in his quest to keep the country together and fight for human rights.

He wasn't flashy or smooth and he certainly sounded funny at times, but he had the smarts to get into power, stay in charge, and get a lot done.

By strategically playing the "I'm just an ordinary guy" card, the little scrapper from Shawinigan stayed ahead of the game and remained a big man in Canadian politics.

collection as having been given to him by various world leaders. Jean's challenge: could Canada do any less? This stunt left everyone chuckling and wondering what the fuss was all about. The master had scored another victory.

Timeline: The life and times of Jean Chrétien

YEAR	JEAN'S LIFE	EVENTS IN CANADA AND THE WORLD
1934	Jean is born in Shawinigan, Quebec, on January 11.	
1935		The Bank of Canada is established.
1936		The Canadian Broadcasting Corporation (CBC) is created.
1939	Jean is sent away to a boarding school, Jardin de l'Enfance.	World War II begins on September 3 (1939–1945). Canada declares war on Germany on September 10.
1940		The National Resources Mobilization Act is introduced. White women are given the right to vote in Quebec. Canada declares war on Italy on June 10.
1941		The unemployment insurance program begins. Japan attacks Pearl Harbor. The Allies declare war on Japan.
1942		The Progressive and Conservative parties unite to become the Progressive Conservative (PC) party. Canada and the United States force citizens of Japanese descent to move inland, away from the west coast.
1944		The Allies land in Normandy, France, on D-Day, June 6.
1945		Germany surrenders on May 8. The family allowance program ("baby bonus") begins. Canada joins the United Nations (UN). The United States drops two atomic bombs on Japan. Japan surrenders on September 2.
1946	Extreme frostbite paralyzes the left side of Jean's face. He is sent to his second boarding school, called Joliette.	
1947		The Canadian Citizenship Act is implemented.
1948		William Lyon Mackenzie King resigns as prime minister. Louis St. Laurent becomes the 12th prime minister of Canada. South Africa introduces apartheid. A war (1948–1949) between Israel and Arab forces from Egypt, Syria, Transjordan (later Jordan), Lebanon, and Iraq begins.
1949		Newfoundland joins Canada. Canada joins the North Atlantic Treaty Organization (NATO).
1950		The Korean War begins: North Korea invades South Korea.
1952		Queen Elizabeth II is crowned.
1954	Jean's mother, Marie, dies.	
1955	Jean earns a BA from St. Joseph Seminary in Trois-Rivières, PQ.	
1956		The Suez War takes place: Great Britain and France attack Egypt to maintain international control of the Suez Canal.
1957	Jean marries Aline Chaîné.	John Diefenbaker becomes Canada's 13th prime minister. Ellen Fairclough becomes Canada's first female cabinet minister. Lester B. Pearson wins the Nobel Peace Prize. The USSR launches the first two earth satellites: Sputnik I and II. The Vietnam War begins (1957–1975): North Vietnam attacks South Vietnam and wins control of it.

More on the life and times of Jean Chrétien

YEAR	JEAN'S LIFE	EVENTS IN CANADA AND THE WORLD
1958	Jean receives a law degree from Laval University and is called to the Quebec bar. His daughter, France, is born.	James Gladstone is appointed Canada's first First Nations senator. The CBC begins coast-to-coast TV broadcasts.
1959	Jean and his family move back to Shawinigan.	Georges Vanier is the first French-Canadian governor general. Fidel Castro becomes premier and dictator of Cuba.
1960		First Nations peoples are granted the right to vote. The Canadian Bill of Rights is passed.
1961		The CCF party changes its name to the New Democratic Party. The Berlin Wall is built.
1962	Jean is appointed director of the bar of Trois-Rivières, Quebec (1962–1963).	The last execution takes place in Canada. US president Kennedy orders a naval blockade of Cuba, bringing the world to the brink of nuclear war.
1963	Jean is elected to the House of Commons at the age of 29. His son, Hubert, is born.	Lester B. Pearson becomes Canada's 14th prime minister. The Royal Commission on Bilingualism and Biculturalism begins. US president Kennedy is assassinated in Dallas, Texas.
1964		Nelson Mandela is jailed for opposing apartheid in South Africa.
1965		The Maple Leaf flag is adopted.
1966	Jean is assistant to Prime Minister Lester B. Pearson. He is appointed parliamentary secretary to Minister of Finance Mitchell Sharp.	Universal medical care is established in Canada. The CBC begins colour television broadcasts. Indira Gandhi becomes prime minister of India.
1967	He joins the cabinet as minister without portfolio.	Canada celebrates the 100th anniversary of Confederation. French president Charles de Gaulle visits Montreal and exclaims "Vive le Québec libre" ("Long live free Quebec"). Israel fights Egypt, Jordan, and Syria in the Six Day War.
1968	Jean becomes minister of national revenue, then minister of Indian affairs and northern development (1968–1974). His adopted son, Michel, is born.	Lincoln MacCauley Alexander becomes the first black MP. Pierre Elliott Trudeau becomes Canada's 15th prime minister. René Lévesque founds the separatist Parti Québécois. US civil rights leader Martin Luther King is assassinated.
1969		Parliament and federal institutions are made officially bilingual. New Brunswick is the first province to be officially bilingual. US astronaut Neil Armstrong walks on the moon.
1970		Front de libération du Québec (FLQ) terrorists kidnap two officials. The War Measures Act is passed, suspending civil liberties.
1974	Jean becomes president of the Treasury Board (1974–1976).	US president Nixon resigns due to the Watergate scandal: he tried to cover up a break-in at the rival Democratic party headquarters.
1976	Jean becomes minister of industry, trade, and commerce (1976–1977).	The summer Olympics are held in Montreal. The first Parti Québébois government is elected in Quebec.
1977	Jean becomes minister of finance (1977–1979).	Canadian road signs are changed to show distances and speed limits in metric.
1979		Joe Clark becomes the 16th prime minister of Canada. Margaret Thatcher becomes the first female prime minister of Great Britain.

Still more on the life and times of Jean Chrétien

YEAR		JEAN'S LIFE	EVENTS IN CANADA AND THE WORLD
1980		Jean is appointed minister of justice and attorney general of Canada, minister of state for social development, and minister responsible for constitutional negotiations (1980–1982).	The Quebec referendum on sovereignty is held: the "no" vote wins. Jeanne Sauvé is appointed the first female speaker of the House of Commons. Terry Fox's Marathon of Hope takes place (April 12–September 2). "O Canada" becomes the official national anthem of Canada.
1981		Jean's father, Wellie, dies.	The French-language sign law of Quebec comes into effect. Terry Fox dies on June 28.
1982		Jean appoints Bertha Wilson as the first female justice of the Supreme Court of Canada. Jean becomes minister of energy, mines, and resources (1982–1984).	The first known cases of Acute Immune Deficiency Syndrome (AIDS) are reported in Canada. The Canada Act is passed: the constitution is brought home to Canada and the Charter of Rights and Freedoms becomes law. The Assembly of First Nations is formed.
1983			Bertha Wilson is Canada's first female Supreme Court justice. Jeanne Sauvé is appointed the first female governor general. The Internet is created.
1984		Jean loses the Liberal leadership race to John Turner. He becomes deputy prime minister, secretary of state for external affairs, and minister responsible for the Francophonie. Jean becomes critic for external affairs.	Aboriginal languages are recognized as official languages in the Northwest Territories. John Turner becomes the 17th prime minister of Canada (June 30, 1984–September 17, 1984). Brian Mulroney becomes Canada's 18th prime minister. Marc Garneau becomes the first Canadian to go into outer space. The Bhopal disaster occurs in India: a chemical leak from a pesticide plant kills over 2,000 people and injures up to 600,000.
1985		Jean's autobiography, *Straight from the Heart*, is published.	Air India Flight 182, from Toronto, is blown up over the Atlantic Ocean, killing 329 passengers; 280 Canadians are killed. Amendments are made to the Indian Act to include the right of First Nations peoples to self-government.
1986		Jean leaves politics to practise law (1986–1990).	Canada denounces South Africa's apartheid government. The USSR launches the Mir space station.
1987			Provincial premiers agree to the Meech Lake Accord. Frobisher Bay, Northwest Territories, changes its name to Iqaluit.
1988			Calgary hosts the winter Olympics.
1989			The $1 bill is replaced with the $1 coin. A massacre occurs at L'école polytechnique in Montreal: 14 female engineering students are killed. Tiananmen Square protests lead to a massacre in Beijing, China. In Germany, the Berlin Wall is torn down.
1990		Jean is elected leader of the Liberal Party of Canada. He becomes leader of the Opposition (1990–1993).	The Oka crisis takes place in Quebec: Mohawks barricade the road to Oka to protest a golf course being built on burial grounds. The Meech Lake Accord fails in the Manitoba legislature. The Bloc Québécois party forms. Nelson Mandela is freed from prison in South Africa. Iraq invades Kuwait, which starts the Gulf War (1990–1991).
1991			The Goods and Services Tax (GST) is introduced. Canadian forces enter the Gulf War against Iraq. Julius Alexander Isaac becomes the first black chief justice of the Supreme Court of Canada. The USSR collapses as countries declare independence.

Even more on the life and times of Jean Chrétien

YEAR	JEAN'S LIFE	EVENTS IN CANADA AND THE WORLD
1992		Roberta Bondar becomes the first Canadian woman in space. The Charlottetown Accord is rejected in a referendum. The Socialist Federal Republic of Yugoslavia ceases to exist. Members of the Canadian Airborne Regiment are sent to Somalia.
1993	Jean becomes Canada's 20th prime minister (1993–2003).	Shidane Arone, a Somali youth, is beaten to death by members of the Canadian Airborne Regiment. Kim Campbell becomes the first female prime minister of Canada. Czechoslovakia divides into Slovakia and the Czech Republic.
1994		The North Atlantic Free Trade Agreement (NAFTA) between Canada, Mexico, and the United States comes into effect. A genocide occurs in Rwanda between Hutus and Tutsis. South Africa holds its first fully multiracial elections.
1995	An intruder breaks into Jean's home during the night.	The Airborne Regiment is disbanded due to 1993's Somali affair. A plebiscite is held by the Cree of Quebec: a huge majority favours remaining part of Canada. A second referendum on separation from Canada is held in Quebec: the "no" vote wins again by a slim margin. Canadian peacekeepers are sent to Bosnia. Dr. Bernard A. Harris Jr. becomes the first black American astronaut to walk in space.
1996		Dolly the sheep, the first mammal to be successfully cloned from an adult cell, is born.
1997	Jean is re-elected for a second term as prime minister.	The constitutional reform known as the Calgary Declaration is accepted by all provincial and territorial leaders, except Quebec's.
1998	Jean makes an official visit to Cuba.	The Supreme Court rules that Quebec cannot legally separate from Canada without the approval of the federal government. Google Inc. is founded.
1999		Nunavut, Canada's third territory, is formed. The Euro currency is introduced in European Union countries.
2000	Jean receives an honourary doctorate from Memorial University in St. John's, Newfoundland. He is re-elected for a third term as prime minister.	The Reform party is replaced by the Canadian Alliance. Former prime minister Pierre Elliott Trudeau dies.
2001		Canada becomes the first country to legalize medicinal marijuana. In the United States, an estimated 3,000 people are killed in terrorist attacks on September 11, 2001. American, Australian, and British troops invade Afghanistan. Canadian troops are committed to go to Afghanistan.
2002		Canada signs the Kyoto Protocol to reduce greenhouse gases.
2003	Jean steps down as prime minister.	Paul Martin becomes Canada's 21st prime minister. Severe Acute Respiratory Syndrome (SARS) hits Toronto. The Iraq war begins: land troops from the United States, United Kingdom, Australia, and Poland invade Iraq.
2004	He returns to practising law.	Testimony begins at the Gomery Commission's inquiry into the sponsorship scandal. Tsunami tidal waves sweep across much of the coastlines of southeast Asia, killing at least 290,000 people.
2005	Jean testifies at the Gomery inquiry about the sponsorship scandal.	Michaëlle Jean becomes Canada's first black governor general.

49

Glossary: words and facts you might want to know

auditor general: officially examines the accounts of the federal government's departments, agencies, and many of its corporations. The auditor general is independent of the government and reports the results of yearly audits to the House of Commons. The auditor general must also report on whether the public money has been spent economically and efficiently.

Bouchard, Lucien (1938–): lawyer, former Canadian ambassador to France. He was a Conservative MP from Quebec when he formed the federal separatist party Bloc Québécois in 1990. He disagreed with the Meech Lake Accord, which was being negotiated with all the provinces. He campaigned during the Quebec referendum of 1995 to have Quebecers vote to separate from Canada. In 1996, he switched to Quebec provincial politics as leader of the Parti Québécois and premier of the province. Disappointed with the progress of Quebec's separation, he resigned from politics in 2001.

British North America Act: law enacted on March 29, 1867, by the British Parliament to confederate (unite) the colonies of the Province of Canada, Nova Scotia, and New Brunswick. It came into effect on July 1, 1867. In 1982, it was renamed the Constitution Act, 1867, as part of the patriation (bringing home) of Canada's constitution.

cabinet minister: a member of the legislature (House of Commons or Senate) who has been invited by the prime minister to head a major government department or ministry of state. The cabinet acts as a unit; any opinion expressed by a minister is that of the whole cabinet.

Campbell, Avril Phaedra Douglas (Kim) (1947–): Canada's first female and 19th prime minister (June 25–November 4, 1993). Kim was elected leader of the Progressive Conservative party in 1993, but quickly lost her seat and the position of prime minister as her party was reduced to two seats in the House of Commons. She retired from politics and is now involved in the promotion of democracy around the world.

Charter of Rights and Freedoms: part of the Canadian Constitution (the highest laws in the country), which came into effect in 1982. It is meant to protect citizens from the government. It also protects minorities from parliamentary majorities. The Canadian charter covers several fields: fundamental rights, democratic rights, mobility rights, legal rights, equality rights, and language rights. All laws in the country that do not agree with the charter have no power.

Chrétien, Aline Chaîné (1936–): wife of Jean Chrétien. They were married in 1957 and have three children: France, Hubert, and Michel. She is fluent in Italian, Spanish, English, and French.

Clark, Charles Joseph (Joe) (1939–): Canada's 16th prime minister (1979–1980). He was only 39 years old when he led a minority government, making him the youngest prime minister in Canada's history. His term as prime minister lasted only eight months and he was replaced as leader of the Progressive Conservative party by Brian Mulroney in 1983.

Clarkson, Adrienne (1939–): governor general and commander-in-chief of Canada from 1999 to 2005. Born in Hong Kong, she and her family came to Canada in 1942, during the war, as refugees. After graduating from university with bachelor's and master's degrees in English literature, and completing post-graduate work at the Sorbonne in Paris, she was host, writer, and producer of television shows for many years. She served as agent general of Ontario in Paris, promoting Ontario's business and cultural interests in Europe. She was also president and publisher of McClelland & Stewart, and has written and directed several films.

Clinton, William Jefferson Blythe IV (Bill) (1946–): 42nd president of the United States (1992–2000). He won a prestigious Rhodes scholarship to Oxford University and earned a law degree before starting a career in politics.

constitution: the highest set of laws in a country. Just like you have rules in your home to help take care of your property, relationships, and personal well-being, a constitution is a set of laws or rules that lays out how a government must take care of its people, and the rights these people can expect their government to protect. Most countries have written constitutions that set out the basic laws of their state.

Copps, Sheila (1952–): in 1993, first woman to be named deputy prime minister. Sheila entered politics in 1981 after working as a newspaper journalist. She has held the cabinet positions of minister of the environment and minister of heritage. She ran twice for the leadership of the Liberal party, in 1990 and 2003. She left politics in 2004.

Duplessis, Maurice LeNoblet (1890–1959): lawyer, premier of Quebec (1936–1939, 1944–1959), and leader of the now-defunct Union Nationale party. He was a controversial politician, seen as anti-union and against people having basic rights and freedoms. However, under his leadership the Quebec government balanced its books 15 years in a row, even as it

For more information on the terms listed in this glossary, visit www.jackfruitpress.com

More words and facts you might want to know

launched huge public works, including highway and hydroelectric projects, and university, school, and hospital construction.

Fetal Alcohol Syndrome (FAS): a group of physical and mental defects that a baby may develop when a mother drinks alcohol during pregnancy. When a pregnant woman drinks alcohol, so does her baby; alcohol passes through the placenta right into the fetus. The baby may suffer lifelong effects as a result, such as brain damage, facial deformities, and growth deficits. Heart, liver, and kidney defects also are common, as well as vision and hearing problems. People with FAS may have trouble learning, paying attention, remembering things, and problem-solving.

First Nations peoples: the descendants of the first inhabitants of North America. The constitution recognizes three separate groups of aboriginal people: Indians, Métis, and Inuit. Each group has unique heritages, languages, cultural practices, and spiritual beliefs.

governor general: the representative of the king or queen in Canada who provides the royal assent necessary for all laws passed by Parliament. The governor general is a figurehead who performs only symbolic, formal, ceremonial, and cultural duties, and whose job is to encourage Canadian excellence, identity, unity, and leadership. Governors general are Canadian citizens appointed for terms of approximately five years. During their term, they live and work in the official residence of Rideau Hall in Ottawa, parts of which are open to the public as a historic site, art gallery, and educational centre.

Grits: nickname of the Liberal party. The name comes from the grit or fine sand that is used as an abrasive, like sandpaper. It comes from a slang term, "true grit," which means to have a strong character and not back down when the going gets tough. "Clear Grits" was first used in Canada in 1849 to describe the progressive members of the Reform Party of Upper Canada, who pushed for fair and responsible government. Their motto was "all sand and no dirt, clear grit all the way through." The Clear Grits joined with reformers from Lower Canada (the Parti rouge) to create the Liberal party.

King, Dr. Martin Luther (1915–1968): African-American Baptist minister and a leader of the civil rights movement in the United States. He believed that every person was equal, no matter what their skin colour was or if they were rich or poor. He led peaceful demonstrations to try to change the way black and poor people were treated by the rest of society. He was shot and killed in Memphis, Tennessee, while leading sanitation workers in a protest against low wages and intolerable working conditions.

Laurier, Sir Wilfrid (1841–1911): Canada's seventh prime minister (1896–1911) and the first one who was a French Canadian.

Lévesque, René (1922–1987): journalist and premier of Quebec (1976–1985). A former Liberal member of the Quebec National Assembly, he founded the Parti Québécois in 1968 because he disagreed with the Liberal party's stand on how Quebec fit into Canada. His government's Bill 101 made French the official language of Quebec. In 1980, he was defeated in a referendum on whether Quebec should split from Canada while maintaining a sovereignty association with it.

Liberal Party of Canada: political party that adopted its name after Confederation in 1867. It was formed from the union of the pre-Confederation Reform party (of what is now Ontario) and Parti rouge (in present-day Quebec).

majority government: when the governing party holds more seats than all other parties combined.

Martin, Paul Edgar Philippe Jr. (1938–): 21st prime minister of Canada (2003–present). Prior to entering politics, Paul was a business executive in Quebec firms. His father, Paul Martin Sr., had been a cabinet minister and candidate for the leadership of the Liberal party.

McLachlin, Madam Chief Justice Beverley (1943–): first female chief justice of the Supreme Court of Canada, since 2000. After completing her bachelor's and master's degrees in philosophy, she studied law and was called to the bar of Alberta in 1969 and the bar of British Columbia in 1971. She was a professor of law before beginning her career as a judge in 1981.

McLellan, Anne (1950–): lawyer and politician. Since December 2003, she has been the deputy prime minister of Canada and minister of public safety and emergency preparedness. She has served in many cabinet positions: minister of natural resources and federal interlocutor for Métis and non-status Indians; minister of justice and attorney general of Canada; and minister of health.

member of Parliament (MP): politician who is elected to sit in the House of Commons. During a general election, the country is divided up into ridings (or constituencies). The voters in each riding elect one candidate to represent them in the government as their MP.

More words and facts you might want to know

Mulroney, Martin Brian (1939–): 18th prime minister of Canada (1984–1993). Brian was born in Quebec to Irish immigrants, and trained as a lawyer. He specialized in labour negotiations and eventually became president of a mining company. Without ever having run for office, Brian became leader of the Progressive Conservative party in 1983. In 1984, he led the PC party to win 211 seats, the most in Canadian history.

national deficit: the amount that the government's spending exceeds its income in a year. If the government doesn't have any savings, it has to borrow money to pay for its programs. This is called "going into debt." Borrowing money costs even more money because the government has to make interest payments to the institution that lent it the money. The opposite of a deficit is a surplus. This is when the government spends less than it collects in revenue. Only when there is a surplus can the government begin to pay off its debt.

non-confidence vote: a special vote in the House of Commons that a minority government must win to stay in power. If the government does not win the vote, it has lost the confidence of the House. The government usually resigns or asks the governor general to dissolve Parliament and call an election. Votes on the speech from the throne and tax and spending bills are automatically considered to be non-confidence votes. Voting on any major bill that reflects the government's program can be, too. The Opposition can also introduce a minor motion or an amendment to a motion that explicitly says the government does not have the confidence of the House. The House then votes on it.

Parliament Hill: in Ottawa, Ontario. It is the site of Canada's federal government buildings. The House of Commons, the Senate, the offices of many members of Parliament, and committee rooms are housed here. It is a complex of buildings that sits above the Ottawa River. Building began in 1859, and it was officially opened in 1866. It was destroyed by a fire and rebuilt in 1916.

Pearson, Lester Bowles (1897–1972): Canada's 14th prime minister (1963–1968). He was a man of several careers before he entered politics, including history professor, secretary in the Canadian High Commission in London during World War II, ambassador to the United States, and deputy minister of external affairs. He attended the founding conference of the United Nations and worked to have Canada join NATO. He received the Nobel Peace Prize in 1957.

Progressive Conservative (PC) party: the name of the Conservative Party of Canada following its union with some members of the farm-focused Progressive party in 1942. The Conservative party began in 1854, when politicians from Upper and Lower Canada joined to form a coalition government of the Province of Canada. Sir John A. Macdonald was its first leader. In 2004, the party merged with the Canadian Alliance to become the new Conservative party.

Quebec referendum: in the first of two, the Parti Québécois government asked the people of Quebec in 1980 if they wanted to separate from the rest of Canada. The concept was rejected by 60 per cent of Quebecers, although it's estimated that 50 per cent of Francophones in the province supported it. The second referendum was held in 1995. Once again, separation was defeated by 50.1 per cent of the people.

Queen Elizabeth II (1926–): Queen of the United Kingdom, Canada, and her other Realms and Territories, Head of the Commonwealth, Defender of the Faith. She succeeded to the throne following her father's death in 1952. She proclaimed Canada's constitution in 1982.

question period: a practice in the House of Commons in which members of Parliament ask government ministers, including the prime minister, questions. It lasts 45 minutes.

Quiet Revolution (1960–1966): or *Révolution tranquille*, a time when Quebec experienced much change. The Quebec Liberal party introduced reforms to modernize the province after 24 years under the leadership of the Union Nationale party, a party that held on tightly to outdated, old-fashioned values. A new age of open debate took place when every policy was examined.

separatists: people or groups of people in Quebec who wish to separate from Canada. Support for separating grew quickly in the late 1960s and 1970s, especially after the Parti Québécois started in 1968. By 1976, the PQ party was in power in Quebec and working on a referendum to ask the people if they wanted independence from Canada.

September 11, 2001: also known as 9/11, the day in 2001 when suicide bombers hijacked four commercial airplanes and used them as bombs. They crashed two into the twin towers of the World Trade Center (one per tower), in New York City, causing them to collapse, and a third into the US Department of Defence headquarters, the Pentagon, just outside of Washington, DC. The fourth hijacked plane crashed into a field in Pennsylvania after passengers fought the hijackers.

Still more words and facts you might want to know

Social Credit party: a former federal party. It exists still as a provincial party in British Columbia. From 1935 to 1968, the federal Social Credit party sent members to Parliament, mainly from Alberta, British Columbia, and Quebec. It believed the government should give people money so they could afford to buy goods and services available in the community. This money was called "social credit."

spin doctors: people who are hired to put a positive slant on a news event or newsworthy person. The interpretation they give is often heavily biased and intended to protect or defend their client from criticism. They are also known as publicists or public-relations agents. An example of what a spin doctor does is helping a person who is running in an election. Perhaps the candidate stutters, trips over his words all the time, or isn't able to express himself very well. The spin doctor may turn this around, or "put a spin on it," by saying that this way of talking shows that the candidate is a "man of the people." This may make voters like him even more.

sponsorship scandal (1995–): charges of corruption against the Liberal government that an estimated $100 million went to Liberal-friendly advertising agencies, public-relations firms, and other middlemen who often delivered shoddy work, or no work at all. Some of this money may have found its way back into the Liberal party's hands. Following the Quebec referendum in 1995, the federal government began the national unity program to advertise how great Canada is. The government sponsored sports and cultural events, films, TV and radio, books, magazines, and many other projects. The scandal dominated the proceedings of the House of Commons from 2002, when it was first discovered.

Supreme Court of Canada: the highest court for all legal issues since 1949. The court is made up of a chief justice (judge) and eight junior judges. It advises the federal and provincial governments about interpreting the constitution. It is also a court of appeal for criminal and civil cases.

Team Canada: a partnership of the federal, provincial, and territorial governments, and Canada's business community. Participants work together, travelling to foreign countries to increase trade, investment, and jobs for Canadians. Each Team Canada mission is led by the PM.

Tories: nickname of the Conservative party in both Great Britain and Canada. It comes from the Irish word *tóraidhe*, which means pursuer or chaser. The term was originally used by the British to degrade the Roman Catholic Irish who robbed the English settlers and soldiers in Ireland. From 1689, it has been the name of the political party with conservative ideas and, later, as the party that is closely associated with the Church of England (Anglican Church).

Trudeau, Pierre Elliott (1919–2000): 15th prime minister of Canada (1968–1979, 1980–1984). Pierre worked as a lawyer and professor before he entered politics in 1965.

Turner, John Napier (1929–): Canada's 17th prime minister (June 30–September 17, 1984). John was born in Great Britain but raised in Canada. He became a lawyer and was recruited into the Liberal Party of Canada. His term as prime minister lasted 80 days.

24 Sussex Drive: in Ottawa, the official residence of the prime minister of Canada since 1951. The house was built in 1866 by mill owner and member of Parliament Joseph Mer-rill Currier as a wedding gift to his bride, Hannah. He called the home "Gorffwysfa," a Welsh word meaning "place of peace."

Union Nationale: originally a coalition political party made up of the Quebec Conservative party and the Action Libéral Nationale party. It was formed in 1935 to defeat the Quebec Liberal party in the election that year. It lost, but it won the election the next year under the leadership of Maurice Duplessis. The party professed to be protectors of Quebec's rights within Canada. It last held power in 1970.

United Nations (UN): an organization that works for international peace and security. The UN provides a place for representatives of countries to meet and settle their problems peacefully. It was established in 1945, at the end of World War II. Its headquarters are in New York City. An office is in Geneva, Switzerland, and agencies can be found throughout the world. Fifty-one countries joined the UN when it started (including Canada and the United States) and over 70 more have signed on since then.

For more information on the terms listed in this glossary, visit www.jackfruitpress.com

Index